Bamboo Valley

A Story of a Chinese Bamboo Forest

The
Nature
Conservancy®

To Kirit — A.W. H.

For my wife, Debbie, and daughters, Jenna and Ariana — J.E.

Text copyright © 1997 Ann Whitehead Nagda.
Illustrations copyright © 1997 Jim Effler.
Book copyright © 1997 Trudy Corporation, 353 Main Avenue, Norwalk, CT 06851.

Soundprints is a division of Trudy Corporation, Norwalk, Connecticut.

Book Design: Shields & Partners, Westport, CT

First Edition 1997
10 9 8 7 6 5 4 3 2
Printed in Hong Kong

Acknowledgments:
   Our very special thanks to the staffs of the National Zoological Park in Washington DC, especially Lisa Stevens, for their review and guidance.

Library of Congress Cataloging-in-Publication Data

Nagda, Ann Whitehead

Bamboo valley: a story of a Chinese bamboo forest / by Ann Nagda ;
illustrated by Jim Effler.
          p.   cm.
Summary: A panda encounters danger as he leaves his Chinese bamboo forest
in search of a new home.
          ISBN 1-56899-491-5 (hardcover)   ISBN 1-56899-492-3 (pbk.)
1. Giant panda — Juvenile fiction.   [1. Giant panda — Fiction.   2. Pandas — Fiction.]
I. Effler, James M., ill.   II. Title.
          PZ10.3.N14Bam 1997   97-8677
          [Fic] — dc21   CIP
                                                                AC

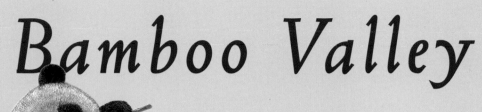

Bamboo Valley

A Story of a Chinese Bamboo Forest

by Ann Whitehead Nagda
Illustrated by Jim Effler

Soundprints™
Where Children Discover...

In a bamboo thicket high in the mountains of central China, all is quiet except for the steady patter of rain. Low clouds stretch ghostly fingers into the forests. The slopes are wrapped in milky mist. Beneath towering fir and spruce trees, arrow bamboo grows six feet high. The autumn rain slides off the bamboo leaves and drips onto the fur of a sleeping panda.

The two-year-old panda left his mother several months ago and now must find his own home range, a small patch of land that can provide food, water, and shelter from heavy rains.

Awakening from his nap, the panda yawns and reaches for a bamboo stem. But the stem in front of him sways and slowly disappears into the ground. A bamboo rat has stolen it. With strong, sharp teeth, the rat cut the stem and pulled it through the roof of one of its many underground tunnels. There, in the dark safety of the tunnel, the bamboo rat nibbles contentedly.

To get away from the troublesome rat, the panda moves to another bamboo patch and sits down. With his back resting against a mossy rock, he pulls a bamboo stem to his mouth and nips off leaves and branch tips. He hears a snort. A large female panda runs to him, roaring. She is not willing to share her home area with him. She slaps him with her paw. The young male turns his head away and covers his black eye patches with his paws to show that he doesn't want to fight. He moans and then moves away. She huffs and walks to a hollow tree nearby. Her infant, hidden inside the giant fir, squawks as she enters.

The panda crosses a stream and finds another stand of arrow bamboo, but all the leaves and stalks are brown and brittle. He chews on a stem, but it doesn't satisfy his hunger. Much of the arrow bamboo in these mountains flowered in the spring for the first time in 45 years, producing many seeds. After flowering, the bamboo died. This spells trouble for the panda — he must find a home range with live bamboo.

The panda lumbers down the mountain and enters a forest of oak, beech, and maple trees. Autumn has colored their leaves orange, red, and gold. Thick stalks of umbrella bamboo grow here and the panda grabs a mouthful of leaves. While he rests against an oak tree, acorn shells drop beside him. A moon bear with a white crescent on its chest stands in a tree fork. The bear peels acorns with its teeth, spits out shells, and eats nut kernels. To prepare for winter hibernation, the moon bear must eat up to 12,000 acorns each day. Looking down, the fierce moon bear utters a low growl and the panda scrambles away.

Daylight is fading as the panda emerges from the forest onto the lower slopes of the mountain. All the trees are gone, cut down by farmers who grow crops here. Late in the night, the panda approaches one of the stone houses in the village. Ears of corn hang to dry below the eaves of the roof. The panda sniffs them, but more interesting smells come from the kitchen. He pushes open the door and finds a pot of leftover rice and pork bones beside the stove. With his strong jaws, he crushes the bones as easily as he crushes tough stalks of bamboo.

The farmer and his wife wake up to the sound of crashing pots and pans. They wave blankets to chase the panda out of their house.

The next morning, a farmer leaves his lunch
unguarded while he harvests corn near a river.
The panda finds the lunch of mantou wrapped in
a cloth. While the panda eats the steamed bread,
he hears barking. Startled, he spots a pack of five
Asian wild dogs racing toward him. The panda
looks around in terror. There are no trees for him
to climb to safety. He runs to the swiftly flowing
river and plunges into the ice cold water. He swims
with a sturdy dog-paddle, but the river
carries him downstream.

Climbing out on the opposite bank, the panda shakes himself off. The dogs pace and whine on the other side, but don't enter the icy water. The panda hurries uphill to a forest of birch. Safe now in the forest, the panda stops to drink from the turquoise waters of a mountain stream. A Darjeeling woodpecker flies overhead, lands on a tree, and begins to drill the trunk with a sharp rata-tat-tat. Suddenly the panda is startled by the sound of dead branches snapping and crashing. Seventy long-haired golden monkeys leap from tree to tree. They stop to pick lichens from the birch branches, then noisily move on.

Snow begins to fall from low, leaden clouds. The panda is hungry. Although the panda will eat other food when he can get it, he relies on bamboo for most of his diet. It is his only dependable food in winter. He reaches a forest of massive firs and rhododendrons. All the arrow bamboo is dry and brittle. When the panda stops to eat a clump of blackberries, he frightens two tragopan pheasants who dart away and hide under a rhododendron bush.

The panda shuffles on, covering several miles without finding anything to eat. He passes a large takin bull munching on the leathery leaves of a rhododendron bush. A nuthatch digs in the snow and finds a cache of pine seeds he hid weeks ago. Buried seeds that the nuthatch doesn't eat will sprout in the spring and grow into new pine trees.

After hours of plodding through the deepening snow, the panda stops to gnaw on some tree bark. Trees become stunted as the panda continues upward. He reaches a pass at 12,000 feet. Below him lies another valley. If he doesn't find the bamboo soon, he may starve.

Large flakes of snow swirl around him as he heads steadily downhill. In the dim light of late afternoon, he enters a forest of fir. Stone bamboo grows beneath the sheltering roof of fir and spruce branches. Wet snow clings to stems and leaves, bending bamboo stalks toward the ground. A bamboo rat peers at him with beady eyes. Stuffing a bamboo stem into its burrow, the rat disappears underground as well.

The panda sits down inside the bamboo thicket and stuffs tender green leaves into his mouth. He fills his empty stomach. Satisfied for the first time in days, he falls asleep.

Just before dawn, the panda eats again. By daybreak, he is thirsty. He toboggans downhill on his chest and stomach through deep snow. He hears the gurgling of a mountain stream and climbs over snow-covered boulders to drink the icy water. Downstream, he finds more lush bamboo. Lying on a bed of dry needles under a tall fir, he pulls bamboo stems to his mouth and eats and eats. In this new valley, the panda has found a place to call home.

Asian Bamboo Forest

Giant pandas used to roam over a much larger area of China than they do today, as well as northern parts of Burma, Thailand, and Vietnam. Now giant pandas are found only in a few small mountainous areas of China.

About the Asian Bamboo Forest

For one million years, giant pandas have roamed the bamboo forests of Asia. During the past century, bamboo forests have been cut down at an alarming rate. As the population of China exploded — with 1.2 billion people in an area about the size of the United States , it's the most populous country on earth — forests were chopped down so that people could grow food, have pastures for their animals, build homes, and make fires to keep themselves warm. Even in protected nature reserves, local peasants still go into the forests to get firewood.

Most kinds of bamboo, including the kinds pandas like, need a moist climate, and bamboo forests are always wet. The actual rainfall is around 40 inches a year, but swirling clouds over this high, mountainous area make the trees drip with moisture. Bamboo is actually a grass, but it can grow many feet tall. Because bamboo remains green and edible all year long, giant pandas have no need to hibernate like moon bears do. Instead, they collect and eat bamboo nearly 14 hours every day, eating as much as 40 pounds of leaves and stems.

Every 40 years, or more, the bamboo that the panda depends on flowers, produces lots of seeds, and then dies. When this happens, not just some plants flower, but most of the plants of the same species all flower at once. The seeds will grow into tiny, new plants the next spring, but it takes several years for them to get big enough to provide sufficient food for pandas. There used to be many species of bamboo available to pandas in the forest, but now that is no longer true. In some places, when the bamboo flowers, the pandas die of starvation.

The Chinese government has set aside many nature reserves to protect the remaining panda habitats, and people caught killing pandas are punished. Despite these measures, the remaining forests are still being cut down and illegal hunting of pandas continues. Today, fewer than 1,000 giant pandas live in a few isolated, mountainous areas of China and every year their number decreases.

Glossary

Asian Birch

Golden Monkey

Asian Nuthatch

Hemlock Spruce

Blackberries

Moon Bear

Darjeeling Woodpecker

Oak and Beech

Dhole, or Asian Wild Dog

Stone Bamboo

 *Arrow Bamboo*

 *Rhododendron*

 *Asiatic Fir*

 *Takin Bull*

 *Bamboo Rat*

 *Tragopan (female)*

Giant Panda

 *Tragopan (male)*